"I'll See You in Court" Supporting Social Justice, Diversity, Equity, and Critical Thinking Through Classroom Management and Discipline in Urban Schools

"I'll See You in Court" Supporting Social Justice, Diversity, Equity, and Critical Thinking Through Classroom Management and Discipline in Urban Schools

Sueanne E. McKinney
Clair T. Berube

INFORMATION AGE PUBLISHING, INC.
Charlotte, NC • www.infoagepub.com

Library of Congress Cataloging-In-Publication Data

The CIP data for this book can be found on the Library of Congress website (loc.gov).

Paperback: 979-8-88730-375-8
Hardcover: 979-8-88730-376-5
E-Book: 979-8-88730-377-2

Copyright © 2023 Information Age Publishing Inc.

All rights reserved. No part of this publication may be reproduced, stored in a retrieval system, or transmitted, in any form or by any means, electronic, mechanical, photocopying, microfilming, recording or otherwise, without written permission from the publisher.

Printed in the United States of America

CONTENTS

Dedications and Recognitions vii

Opening Statements: An Open Letter to
All Urban Educators ix

1. Court is Now in Session 1
2. Creating a Community of Accountable Learners and Citizens 11
3. Law School 25
   William McConnell
4. Court Docket and Jury Selection 33
5. Sentencing 37
6. The Supreme Court 41
   Starrbe Bryant

   Closing Statements 47

   References 49

   Appendix 53

DEDICATIONS AND RECOGNITIONS

I would like to dedicate this book to Ms. Lillian Brinkley, Mrs. Mamie Ratliff, and Mr. Joel Wagner, three of my former principals who not only encouraged this means of Classroom Management and Discipline, but also showed up weekly for our court cases to watch students resolve their conflicts. You all have truly impacted my teaching career.

To Lynne Barrett, my former colleague who made many contributions to this system.

And finally, Dr. Martin Haberman, Dr. Rebecca Bowers, and Delia Stafford-Johnson, my mentors, introduced me to Star Teachers, and how their functions could develop a student-centered Classroom Management and Disciplinary Plan.
—*Sueanne McKinney*

For my Dad, Teddy Thorns, who taught me how to earn respect and how to treat people, especially students.
—*Clair Berube*

To my husband, Theo, and my three children, Sun, Navaj, and Anavya.
—*Starrbe Bryant*

To my wife, Doray, and my two children, Billy and Logan.
—*Dr. Bill McConnell*

OPENING STATEMENTS

An Open Letter to All Urban Educators

Lillian M. Brinkley

As an African American woman who possesses a vast number of firsthand experiences that still resonate in my memories even today, I write this open letter to you for your choice of beginning your journey in one of the most wonderful places in the world—the urban school. Although this may seem contrary to what you may have heard over the course of your preparation and personal experiences, I hope this letter will serve to lessen your anxieties and misunderstandings about what it is like to teach in a high-poverty setting. Take it from one who has been there, you will find this experience to be one of your most rewarding occurrences that you may encounter in your life. It will be a life-changing event for you.

Though you may begin with many perceptions, misperceptions, and myths, several of them are unfounded. Often color tarnishes the foundation of many novice teachers' thinking and beliefs, even though some have not walked through the doors of an urban, high-poverty school. This alone can hamper your chances to become a great teacher, a "Star Teacher" for all of your students-that teacher who changes lives and are remembered by students for a lifetime.

You will learn that the students will see you, not for the color of your skin, but for the love and care you exhibit beyond your instructional skills. You will find

---

"I'll See You in Court" Supporting Social Justice, Diversity, Equity, and Critical Thinking Through Classroom Management and Discipline in Urban Schools, pages ix–x.
Copyright © 2023 by Information Age Publishing
www.infoagepub.com
All rights of reproduction in any form reserved.

children, who if they know through your actions and desires you to want them to learn, they will learn beyond your highest expectations. You will find children who, once they learn that you see beyond the tangibles of what they wear, live, or believe, their love and respect is yours. The children just want to know that you are there to make life better for them and bring hope to their lives and future. Release all of the facades that are often used to justify and solidify why you should not want to teach in an urban school. Know that you can be the teacher who can make the difference and shred the wall between fact and fiction. You may be the one whose commitment to instructing all children can be the difference maker.

As you begin your journey as a teacher in an urban setting, come to accept the truths that dispel you of misconceptions and move toward approaching your task with an open mind, a sound knowledge of history and an understanding of the cultural likeness and differences that make humankind. When you approach each child as the most wonderful child you have ever met when you remove the blindfolds of years of inequality, racism, and untruths, when you see beyond the color of skin, when you respect their values, when you listen, learn, and apply credibility to those attributes that make the child unique, you will know that you have found the job for you---the urban school. Star Teachers reflect this ideology every day.

Know that our schools and the schools in which you will work will be filled with students of many races, colors, beliefs, whose history has been written not by them but for them. Your classroom will be populated by a majority of students with whom you have extraordinarily little understanding or little or no knowledge of their backgrounds, but never forget that the parents are sending us the best they have and trust us to give them the best educational experiences offered. Never forget to reflect on the teaching and learning opportunities that you would want for your child. Strive to give no less to the children in your class. Remove all blinders and show them the respect, love, and attention that you would give to your own. They will love and respect you back. Get to know them. Treat them as if they were the best and they will live up to that expectation. Your classroom will be populated with students you know extraordinarily little about or have never been to their home or neighborhood. But you must be able to look beyond the roadblocks and find the child who can meet success and deserve the best education possible. Remember that the memories that you leave with a child and the experiences of success that you provide will be lasting memories for that child because they know you gave them your best.

Respectfully,
—*Lillian M. Brinkley*
Internationally and Nationally Recognized Principal
National, State, and Local "Principal of the Year"
Past President, NAESP

CHAPTER 1

COURT IS NOW IN SESSION

Can I be an effective classroom manager and disciplining teacher? What are the functions of Star Teachers? Do I have the needed dispositions to be a Star Teacher?

Classroom management and discipline have often been identified by several scholars and educators as the leading cause of attrition in urban, high-poverty school environments. For many novice teachers, erroneous perceptions and beliefs about urban pedagogy and methodology, students, parents, and the community, and their impact on classroom management and discipline, often influence their decision not to teach in an urban district, transfer to another school or district, or leave the profession all together.

> To be an effective educator in an urban school district, begins with building genuine relationships. Relationships will inevitably breed trust. Once trust is established, students will know they are valued for who they are and not their address and will strive to do their best to please the educator, that, in turn, believes in them.
> —Lucy Litchmore

No educator will disagree that teaching in an urban, high-poverty school is a life changing event. Haberman (1995) describes it best: *."... teaching in these situations is an extraordinary life experience—a volatile, highly charged, emotionally draining, physically exhausting experience for even the most competent, experienced teacher"* (1995, p. 1). For

---

"I'll See You in Court" Supporting Social Justice, Diversity, Equity, and Critical Thinking Through Classroom Management and Discipline in Urban Schools, pages 1–10.
Copyright © 2023 by Information Age Publishing
www.infoagepub.com
All rights of reproduction in any form reserved.

the beginner teacher, this description is often inconceivable, and only adds to the emotional intensity and apprehension they sense as they begin their teaching career. It is of great consequence that these beginning teachers are also made aware that thousands of teachers confront copious challenges daily with success, passion, and a desire to have influence and "change student lives."

WHO ARE STAR TEACHERS?

There is no doubt that all individuals have been influenced or impacted by a teacher during their elementary, middle, high school, or even higher education tenure. These are the teachers that are still remembered with admiration and reverence and are often thought in terms of "My favorite teacher." These are the exceptional teachers, the teachers that come to school with fervency and eagerness daily and make learning meaningful and enjoyable for the students. (Haberman, 1995, 2005; Haberman, Gillette, & Hill, 2018) endeared the term "Star Teacher" to describe such educators. According to Haberman, Star Teachers are:

> . . . teachers who, by all common criteria, are outstandingly successful: their students score higher on standardized tests; parents and children think they are great; principals rate them highly, other teachers regard them as outstanding; central office supervisors consider them successful; cooperating universities regard them as superior; and they evaluate themselves as outstanding teachers. (Haberman, 1995, p. 1)

WHAT ARE THE CHARACTERISTICS AND FUNCTIONS OF STAR TEACHERS?

What is it that makes these teachers exceptional in extreme poverty schools? Haberman (1995, 2005) identified 15 characteristics and functions that define a Star Teacher. These characteristics and functions are embedded within their ideology of cultural proficiency and as the foundation for instruction and classroom management and discipline. The mindset of Star Teachers is the appreciation and acceptance of one's culture, and of diversity, equity, and social justice, and then using them to bridge differences in socioeconomic status, heritage, race, handicapping conditions, trauma history and occurrences, and ability levels. The ideology of Star Teachers is a journey—constantly evolving, as Stars relentlessly self-reflect to ensure their personal attitudes, belief systems, and behaviors are free of judgement, bias, and prejudice. Table 1.1 identifies and describes each of the characteristics and functions of Star Teachers as described by Haberman (1995, 2005).

> There should be a Star Teacher in every urban school classroom. These are the teachers who build a sense of family and relationships with their students, and as a result, there are less discipline problems. It's amazing what students are capable of doing just by the simple act of a teacher showing kindness, respect, and concern.
> — Sharon Phillips, Principal

> Students don't care what you know until they know that you care.
> — Sarah Peoples-Perry, Principal

TABLE 1.1. Star Teacher Characteristics and Functions

Characteristic	Description
Protecting Children's Learning	Teachers can capitalize on all learning opportunities.
Persistence	Teachers constantly pursue strategies and activities so that all students can meet success.
Approach to At-Risk Students	Teachers take responsibility for children's learning, regardless of the conditions they face.
Putting Ideas into Practice	Teachers can relate theory and practice.
Professional/Personal Orientation to Students	Teachers expect and can develop rapport with children.
The Bureaucracy	Teachers can adjust and cope with the demands of the bureaucracy.
Fallibility	Techers take responsibility for their own errors and mistakes.
Emotional and Physical Stamina	Teachers can endure the challenges and crises of urban settings.
Organizational Ability	Teachers have extraordinary organizational and managerial skills.
Explanation of Teacher Success	Teachers believe that success is met by effort and challenging work and not by ability alone.
Explanation of Student Success	Teachers are committed to student autonomy and individual differences.
Real Teaching	Teachers engage in active teaching instead of direct instruction.
Making Students Feel Needed	Teachers can make the students feel needed and wanted in the classroom.
Gentle Teaching in a Violent Society	Teacher's ideology is promising, even considering a violent society.
The Material vs. The Student	Teachers find approaches that will assist students in mastering the material.

For the children and youth in poverty from diverse cultural backgrounds who attend urban schools, having effective teachers is a matter of life and death. These children have no life options for achieving decent lives other than by experiencing success in school. For them, the stakes involved in schooling are extremely high. (Haberman, 1995, p. 1; 2018, p. 4)

Being a scholar does not necessarily mean you will be a good teacher or principal. Lots of other qualities and skills and different combinations of qualities are equally important: Compassion for children, organization of classroom, structure and planning, creativity, laughter. Teaching is an art, not a science and teacher dispositions are important.
— Sharon Margulies, Principal

For novice teachers, these characteristics and functions can be developed and matured through a teacher education program, a mentor or master teacher, and/or personal steadfastness and dedication. Most importantly, Star Teachers reveal, display, and express these characteristics and functions through their classroom management and discipline plans and strategies daily.

WHAT IS CLASSROOM MANAGEMENT AND WHY IS IT SUCH A MISUNDERSTOOD TERM?

When pre-service teachers are amid their teacher preparation programs, they study pedagogy, content, theoretical frameworks of human development, technology education and other relevant subject material. However, if you ask them the one aspect of their future profession as a teacher that sends a chill up their spines and increases their anxiety levels, they probably will say classroom management and discipline, especially if they are assigned to an urban, high-poverty school during their practicum or student teaching internship. Teachers know that without a well-managed classroom, nothing of value with instruction and learning can be accomplished. Addressing instruction and classroom management and discipline is one of the most important skills a teacher can possess. While teachers tend to become more proficient at this as time goes by and they mature, all teachers, veterans, and new hires alike, can benefit from techniques that make this task easier and that involve the students in their own agency of classroom management and discipline, especially in urban, high-poverty schools.

> "Just as a "roux" is used as a basic ingredient for gumbo recipes of rich, deep, hearty flavor and texture that is desired, classroom management is the "roux" and heartbeat of an engaged, effective learning environment.
>
> The gradual release of sustained, concurrent teaching processes—social/emotional, real-world life experiences, and academic skills, taught, modeled, practiced, and reviewed, yield well-mannered, independent, self-sufficient scholars who do not need an overseer to maintain order. With the inception of high expectations, time and deposits invested to establish relationships, the teacher is able to plan and deliver effective, engaging instruction to meet the needs of diverse learners as students learn without disorder.
>
> Bythella Denise Taylor Hickman,
> Assistant Principal

What exactly is classroom management and discipline, and why is it such a misunderstood term among educators and scholars alike? Is it forcing children to behave and follow directions? Is it punishment driven by rules and regulations? On the other hand, is it motivating and leading children to achieve their highest potential? Maybe all three? If we think of classroom management and discipline as solely forcing children to behave and act in certain ways or meet punishment, we are missing the interpretation of their roles and significance in the classroom. Reflect on when you were in school; or the last time you were at a presentation you had to attend for work. Was it interesting? Was the presenter personable? Were you engaged or squirming in your seat? School aged children are no different from the rest of us when in similar situations. The teacher effectiveness and ideology of Star Teachers have a lot to do with content competency, pedagogical knowledge, and social-emotional intelligence. Star Teachers are prepared, organized and up on the latest research in the field. They also have open personalities, patience, and wisdom. They know how to lose a battle to win a war. Where do classroom management and discipline come in? The secret is that if a teacher has well thought-out and engaging lesson plans, and consistent procedures in place, the risk of student misbehavior is much lower than with teachers who do not have these skills in practice.

So, what is the difference between these terms and why are they often confused? According to Wong and Wong (2018b) and Haberman (1995, 2005) the terms classroom management and discipline are not synonymous. They are two distinctive terms. Classroom management requires the teacher to think in advance and be initiative-taking. It promotes a sense of responsibility among the students and allows for predictable behavior and actions. If properly implemented and addressed, teaching and learning time is increased. In urban, high-poverty schools, classroom management should also give students a voice and should allow them to participate in the decision-making process grounded through their views and experiences involving authority (Haberman, 2005). Discipline requires the teacher to be reactive; they are responding to a behavior problem that already happened. It involves consequences and punishments, with the major focus on stopping unruly behaviors. Star teachers know this, and because of this understanding, they have fewer discipline problems in the classroom.

According to Myers et al. (2017), the lack of a decent classroom management and discipline plan can be the cause of teacher turnover.

> The most important element of classroom management and discipline in urban schools is the ability to build relationships and relate to students.
> Janna Drof, Teacher, and Counselor

Managing a classroom effectively is a crucial skill teachers need to have in order to maximize academic achievement, enhance student social competence, promote positive classroom climate, and enable supports for students with exceptional needs. In addition, student behavior has a direct effect on teachers' job satisfaction, and an inability to manage students' behavior is likely a key factor in our nation's high turnover rate among teachers, especially in urban, high-poverty schools (e.g., Ingersoll & Smith, 2003; Klassen & Chiu, 2010; Landers et al., 2008, 2004). (Myers et al., 2017, p. 224).

WHAT IS SOCIAL JUSTICE, CULTURALLY RESPONSIVE COMMUNICATION, PROBLEM SOLVING AND CRITICAL THINKING SKILLS, AND WHAT DOES MODERN 21ST CENTURY CLASSROOM MANAGEMENT LOOK LIKE?

Managing a general classroom looks a lot different than it did in earlier decades in American public education. Teachers used to have paddles and switches at the ready to deal with unruly students, with full backing of parents. Federal law prevents this nowadays thankfully, so we have to have higher levels of dealing with classroom management than the bottom rung and lowest level of exerting control, which is fear of physical punishment. There is of course so much more to classroom management and discipline than that. In order to answer the question of what modern classroom management looks like, particularly in urban, high-poverty schools, first we need to describe what modern classrooms in general look like. In the 20th century, up until Brown vs the Board of Education desegregated public schools, children were segregated from each other due to race. There were also no laws in place to protect the constitutional rights of children who were gay, African Americans, or girls for that matter. There was no notion of transgender students or students with different learning styles or learning disabilities. If you were not achieving in the classroom, you were labeled a "dunce" and you were tracked into programs that limited your potential and made it written in stone what your future jobs could be. You could fill a whole book on this issue (and many scholars have) but thanks to the civil rights movement, the disability rights movement, the women's movement and other social movements, children of all social classes are guaranteed certain rights in the public-school classroom with laws to support them.

If you are a college student studying to become a teacher, in the departments and schools of education at your university, you now study topics such as culturally responsive pedagogy, differentiation, Multiple Intelligence Theory, alternative assessments, special education techniques (for general education, not special education teachers) and others. The individual student is the focus, and that means his or her needs are to be met and if one pedagogical technique does not work, you must employ something else. Haberman (1995, 2005) refers to this as Persistence, for urban, high-poverty schools and states that teachers should be capable of employing at least 5–6 techniques or strategies to assist the student in understanding the material. Further, Star Teachers are constantly thinking, "What can I do better?"

Why study these topics? We study them because the world has changed to the degree where people from all over the world always don't stay in their country of origin anymore: we are all free to travel and live elsewhere, and it is easier to do so now than it was 100 or 50 years ago. So how does culture influence classroom management? You would be surprised.

To begin with, what we expect students to behave like can influence our behaviors, which in turn will impact our classroom management and discipline ideology. Should students be talking to each other during instruction? Should our classroom arrangement be organized in rows of student desks? According to Martin (2021),

> What behaviors do we expect from our students, and why? should be a question that every teacher asks themselves as they develop their philosophy and beliefs. In the traditional ensemble ideal, students are attentive, focused, quiet, still, and ready for direction. Those deviating from such norms may be seen as disruptive, disrespectful, or otherwise disengaged—but why do we cast such labels on these students? How might classroom misunderstandings cause harm? In what ways might our behavioral expectations stand at odds with student needs? (para. 1)

Cultural differences, especially with students who are recent immigrants, can show up in communication styles between students and teachers, and can influence how teachers think about student motives, often times, for the worse. This misinterpretation of student behavior can harm a child and can follow them into other classes and grades and sometimes even create insurmountable problems for them. Martin (2021) suggests we examine our biases: "When teachers honestly examine their past experiences and biases, they are less likely to misinterpret the behaviors of culturally different students and treat them inequitably" (para. 14). Past experiences can include both personal and professional circumstances. Teachers must consider the confluence of these experiences to fully unpack the influence on their perspectives. For example, our own experiences as a K–12 student in a white, middle-class community informed what I believed to be "correct" behavior in the ensemble setting. Because we are white and from a middle-class background, our relational style complemented classroom expectations. Years later, as young teachers, we learned that what worked with students at our first position did not necessarily transfer to the classroom in my second position, and in neither case did classroom realities align with my preconceptions about "correct" behavior" (para. 14). We believe that self-reflection or "Teacher Talk" (when teachers face their personal biases; Haberman, 2012) is necessary for successful classroom management and discipline, but teachers should have a keen awareness of culturally responsive pedagogy, as well. Star Teachers know and act upon these daily.

One of the worst outcomes that can be traced to a lack of cultural awareness on behalf of the teacher is the practice of assigning out-of-school suspensions, or any measure of discipline that separates the student from his or her educational opportunities. Students of color receive out of school suspensions at a much higher rate than do white students, and sometimes for the same offenses. According to Del Toro and Wang (2021), research published by the American Psychological Association bears this out: "Overall, researchers found that 26% of the Black students received at least one suspension for a minor infraction over the course of three years, compared with just 2% of white students. Minor infractions included things such as dress code violations, inappropriate language or using a cell phone in class" (para. 3). In recent years, there has been an awareness of this issue and how harmful it is. As a result, teachers who are knowledgeable of cultural differences are turning towards more "restorative" punishments that do not force students to miss school. Star Teachers do not even consider suspension as a discipline option. Their ideology is substantiated by having every student in class feel that they are needed and wanted by them (Haberman, 1995, 2005).

HOW DOES THIS MODEL OF CLASSROOM COURT ADDRESS STUDENT LEADERSHIP AND SELF-DISCIPLINED BEHAVIORS?

21st century classroom management and discipline should incorporate self-governing factors that students can learn, and which can become part of their life-skills beyond the classroom. The goal of adult autonomy is to become self-governed and to be able to do the right thing without threat of punishment. People should behave because it is the right thing to do, not because they will get into trouble if they do not. The Harvard psychologist, Lawrence Kohlberg (1958, 1984) brought this to light with his now famous stages of moral development, which were informed by justice. These were organized into three levels, of which each level has two stages. The levels are pre-conventional, conventional, and post-conventional morality. The stages are: 1) Obedience and punishment, 2) Individual Interest, 3) Social Approval, 4) Authority, 5) Social Contract, and 6) Universal Ethics. Table 1.2 organizes these stages.

Preferably, teachers want students to be functioning at least at the Conventional level where they respect law and order. At the Post-Conventional level, students start to exhibit intrinsic motivational behaviors. They learn for the love of learning and for how it empowers them to direct their lives. Of course, justice has to be tempered by compassion, but when managing a class of youngsters, you can have justice that is fair. Students respect fair teachers, even if they might disagree with them about the rules. The "Classroom Court" model and Star Teachers address these issues.

JUDICIOUS DISCIPLINE

Researcher Paul Gathercoal has developed a theoretical model that he calls "Judicious Discipline" (2001). This theory posits that students should be treated as citizens, and that includes in the classroom as well as in the greater society. This fosters a realization that other people have human rights and that they should develop an interest in rest of society. Human rights guarantee certain things in the United States, including individual rights and responsibilities. These human rights guaranteed by our constitution include "freedom of speech, press, peaceful assembly, and religion; the right to privacy and freedom from unreasonable search and seizure; and the right to due process and equal protection of life, liberty and property" (Gathercoal, 2001, para. 5). Rights of society include state interests, such as property loss and damage, threats to health and safety, educational rights,

TABLE 1.2. Kohlberg's Stages of Moral Development Levels

Levels	Stages	Description
Preconventional	• Obedience and Punishment • Self-Interest (What is in it for me?)	• You behave to avoid punishment. • You scratch my back, I will scratch yours. You obey for a reward.
Conventional	• Interpersonal Conformity • Authority/Law and Order	• Good girl, boy. You behave due to your social norms. • You obey because it is against the law not to.
Post-Conventional	Social Contract Universal Ethical Principles	Social justice. You behave because others have rights too. There is a higher good. Some laws may be bad or corrupt. You behave to meet a higher purpose.

and protection of interference of one's educational attainment (para. 7). Students learn to balance their individual rights with responsibility for the greater society.

According to Gathercoal (2001), "Judicious Discipline" is "front loading;" it doesn't work very well unless expectations are in place and the community of learners develops them. To get started, educators and their students develop classroom and school expectations by rewording the four compelling state interests into positive behavioral statements and then asking the students to help define what they look like in various teaching and learning situations. Table 1.3 below, represents how the compelling state interests can be reworded into positive statements"(Gathercoal, 2001, para. 9).

Gathercoal (2001) describes how we develop character through democratic culture (democratic as in democracy). John Dewey was one of the first educators to speak to democratic culture in schools. His important book *Democracy and Education* (1916) stressed how students should learn how to be good citizens and that learning is social and communal in nature. He was among the first to use the phrase "life-long learners" and stressed how public schools should educate children for their future world, not our world. He said that democracy is not just a political vehicle, but an idea... a theoretical framework (Dewey, 1916). According to Dewey, without democratic principles, the American dream is out of reach. Many educators of the day, and especially Star Teachers, and for decades afterwards, caught on to the idea that character and democracy should be infused into all topics in public education. But is character building only reward and punishment? Gathercoal (2001) does not believe so. Punishment and the avoidance of negative consequences is, according to him, the lowest level on moral development, which is also in alignment with Kohlberg's theory of moral development (Kohlberg, 1984). The notion of classroom culture, democratic practices and justice infuse the "Classroom Court" model in this book and will become clearer in upcoming chapters.

I actually began implementing this model of "Classroom Court" in my classroom in the mid-1980s and had implemented it throughout my career. This model evolved over the years with the assistance and suggestions of my principals, counselors, colleagues, and students. Begin by imagining your classroom being in-

TABLE 1.3. Interest and Behavioral Statements

| The Compelling State Interest and its Positive Behavioral Statement. ||
Compelling State Interest	Positive Behavioral Statements
Threat to Health and Safety	Act in a Safe and Healthy Way
Property Loss and Damage	Treat All Property with Respect
Serious Disruption of the Educational Process	Respect the Rights and Needs of Others
Legitimate Educational Purpose	Take Responsibility for Learning

structed, managed, and disciplined by the creation of an environment that focuses on society, where problem solving, critical thinking, leadership and appropriate classroom behavior is taught through taking their peers to court, holding jobs, and managing money.

CHAPTER 2

CREATING A COMMUNITY OF ACCOUNTABLE LEARNERS AND CITIZENS

How can creating a classroom community assist teachers with classroom management and discipline? How can I hold students accountable for their behavior and assist them in developing into self-disciplined learners? How can I change student behavior instead of reacting to it?

The goal that undergirded this complete transition of my classroom management and discipline plan values, attitudes, and philosophy was that I was spending too much instructional and personal time on it. I aspired to spend less time on classroom management and discipline so that it would free my personal and professional time on planning and instruction. I wanted to plan lessons that were student centered, exciting, and relevant. Although ambitious, this required additional time.

Terminology such as differentiation, culturally responsive pedagogy, social justice, meta-cognition, and mindsets were not introduced to pre-service teachers back in the early 1980s when we both attended our teacher preparation programs, yet this management system addresses each. 'Classroom Court" was based alone on personal creativity, endless discussions with professionals in the field, conversations with my colleagues and family, and input from my students. However, the overall idea of using the judicial system as a means for classroom management and discipline was not my idea. My first principal, Mrs. Mamie Ratliff, informed me that she had read an article about this initiative and wanted me to try it. I did not even get a copy of the article! It has since been updated to include current research, and address the students of today attending urban, high-poverty schools. However, we believe that this model can be used in any type of classroom setting.

We believe that this management and discipline plan also supports the research of Haberman (Haberman, 1991, 1995, 2005, 2012; Haberman et al., 2018) and is aligned with the Star Teacher characteristics. Haberman (2005) explains:

> It is incumbent on teachers to help students see the connections between their life experiences and the content to be learned. But this does not mean limiting the curriculum to the experiences of the students. The very purpose of education is to push students beyond their present understandings-to open their minds and imaginations to the universe of great ideas past, present and future. To do anything less is to lower expectations and standards. Making content relevant by limiting it to students' current life experiences is not meeting students' needs but pandering to ignorance. (p. 68)

DEVELOPING EXPECTATIONS, CONSEQUENCES, AND PROCEDURES

As you read further, you will see I used a variety of theoretical approaches to my Classroom Management and Discipline Model. I used Judicious Discipline, (The learning environment guarantees freedom, justice, and equality; Gathercole, 2004) and Conflict Resolution and Peer Mediation (Solving unresolved conflicts; Crawford & Bodine, 1996) when we held court; Character Education (Incorporating character building lessons and activities; Lickona, 1991) was emphasized by students holding jobs and managing their money; I implemented Positive Classroom Discipline (Strengthening desired behavior while abating inappropriate behavior; Jones, 1987) and Discipline with Dignity (All students should be treated with dignity [Curwin & Mender, 1988]) throughout the entire model.

Although some scholars advocate using the students as assistants when developing the classroom rules, rulemaking can be a complex task, and I always developed my classroom rules during my years of teaching. By doing so, my rules were clear, reasonable, behavior guidelines, and expectations I required of all students so that our classroom could build that sense of community, mindfulness, and self-control. When developing your classroom rules, they should all be measurable; that is, the teacher should be able to determine if a rule has been broken. You should develop at least 5–7 rules, all written in positive terms, and each rule should be modeled and discussed in class of their importance.

Remember that attitudes are not behavioral rules. Statements like "Always have a cheerful outlook" or "Always try your best" are not behavioral classroom rules. They cannot be measured. How can you determine if a student is trying their best? Moreover, a student can complete their work successfully without a cheerful outlook, although it does help.

What happens when a student breaks a classroom rule? Based on my classroom management and discipline ideology, they would experience a consequence. Remember, as mentioned earlier, I wanted to spend less time on classroom management and discipline and spend more time designing and developing exciting lessons for my students. I didn't want to spend my personal time emailing or phoning parents. That was last on my list of options. My colleague at the time, Lynne Barrett, developed an idea

> **Student Reflections**
>
> I am a retired U.S service man, who participated in this classroom management and discipline system over 31 years ago. I had the pleasure of as serving as the Sheriff of "Chill Out" and as a lawyer for one of my peers. I am an introvert by nature but being put in those positions was the beginning of me being able to open up a bit. I was excited to go to school because we did not just learn our lessons from a textbook. We were afforded the opportunity to live out our lessons.
>
> —John Patterson, Former Student
>
> At the time, my favorite parts of the system were pretending to be a lawyer and earning over a million McBucks. Looking back at the classroom management and discipline system when I was in 5th grade, the most valuable aspect was that it kept me engaged in the class. The interrelationships between behavior, attention, and interesting tasks made it easier maintain attention and learn throughout the day.
>
> —Eric Goldman, Former Student

Sample Rules for 5th Grade

Make all your materials needed for learning (e.g., books, notebooks, paper, writing utensils).	Question: Why is this an important rule? What would happen if a student did not bring to class their needed materials?
Raise your hand (our give hand signals) if you must leave your seat during instruction (e.g., sharpening your pencil, throwing trash away).	Question: Why is this rule important? What would happen to our classroom if everyone were able to leave their seat whenever they wanted to?
Respect yourself, your peers, your teacher, your materials, your classroom, and all adults in the building.	Question: What happens to our classroom if you do not show others' respect, or you don't respect your materials or classroom.
Be a good listener (e.g., no interruptions when others are speaking).	Question: What would happen in our classroom if we interrupted each other when talking, and weren't good listeners?
Talking is allowed during identified activities. Make sure you speak using your 12-inch voice, and it is during a permissible time.	Question: What would happen during teaching and learning id you all talked at once?
When in doubt, we'll principal it out!	In certain situations, the principal must be involved if the behavior is not specifically addressed in your rules.

> **Essential Elements of Developing Classroom Rules**
> 1. Limit your behavioral rules between 5–7. Too many rules may be difficult for the students to remember.
> 2. Write your rules in positive terms.
> 3. Make sure your rules are measurable; that is, make sure you can distinguish that a student has broken s rule.
> 4. Make sure your rules exert dignity, as not to embarrass a student.
> 5. Make sure your rules are easy understand so that students know of your expectations.
> 6. Be consistent.
> 7. Make sure your rules and consequences are posted in your classroom and are articulated verbally or in a classroom newsletter to your parents.

of a "Strike System," where we would deal with the majority of discipline consequences in the classroom. "Strike 1" was a Warning. That was also a student job in my classroom-to write the number of strikes students received each day in a notebook. If your district does not allow that, you could simply keep strikes in a notebook yourself. At the beginning of each school year, I would ask the individual students why they received the strike and which classroom rule they broke. This was a means that I would use to help internalize the rules within my students. "Strike 2" required the students to move themselves and their materials to a "Chill Out" area. This area was by no means a deleterious or undignified place to be. It simply was a place where students could regroup, get their thoughts together, and if angry, a place where they could calm down. "Chill Out" contained earphones where they could listen to calming music (Yes, Barry Manilow was one of the selections, as was Mozart, and other easy listening music); it also contained potpourri for a means of aromatherapy. Additionally, "Chill Out" contained literature books about emotions, and how to control them, as well as a mirror. I participated in a professional development activity in which I learned that children do not like to look at themselves when they are angry. While there, students had to complete a Reflection Sheet that required them to analyze the situation, what they could have done differently, how they made me and their peers feel, and what they would do next. Its' intent was to change student behavior. When I had 5 or so minutes, I would do and conference with the student and review their responses on the Reflection Sheet. If they took responsibility for their discipline infraction, they were allowed to rejoin the class. I can still fondly remember a past student, Doug, a red headed boy who frequented "Chill Out." I concluded that he wanted to go to "Chill Out" just to listen to Barry Manilow! There is always that one child in every class! "Strike 3" involved our own Classroom Conduct Notice. We realized that the official school conduct notice required the teacher to write out the situation, and then you had to locate the principal or assistant principal for his/her signature. This required you to leave the classroom and took approximately 20–25 minutes-time that could be spent on instruction. Because of this, we developed our own that only required us to check off the rules that were broken, and our signature. It also contained a brief comment section. If the student forgot to return the Classroom Conduct Notice the next day, they would spend the day in "Chill Out" and a phone call would be made to the parent. My private secretary (classroom job) would file the Reflection Sheets and Classroom Conduct Notice in the student's discipline folders. A copy of the Reflection Sheet and Classroom Conduct Notice is included in the Appendix and can be modified for your grade levels and rules. One critical point I would like to stress is the amount of documentation I acquired in regard to the student's behavior in the classroom. If I ever had to conference with the parents or principal, I had my Strike Notebook, Reflection Sheets, and Classroom Conduct Notices to show the student's behavior, and my interventions to change it.

WHAT ROLE DO PROCEDURES PLAY IN CLASSROOM MANAGEMENT AND DISCIPLINE?

As in society, we are ruled by procedures, or routines that assist us in demonstrating appropriate citizenship (Wong & Wong, 2018a). The National Football League has procedures that the game is organized around, as other sporting events; your family has procedures and routines that govern their households; and there are procedures and routines that preside over the classroom. Wong and Wong (2018b) further state that the number one problem in the classroom is not discipline related, but instead, procedure related (p. 138).

Star Teachers are known for having well thought out classroom procedures that involve Organization, Real Teaching, and You and Me Against the Material, as examples. Their teaching materials and classroom setting are well organized; they don't have to search for materials at the last minute to teach a lesson during instruction. Stars have set procedures for Making Students Feel Needed—if only a phone call to say they were missed when absent.

As a teacher, it is your responsibility to develop the procedures for your classroom, from how students enter the classroom, work in collaborative groups, line up for lunch or dismissal, turning in late or absent work, what to do when they finish their classroom work early, and restroom breaks. These are only a few of the procedures that you must develop for your class. A complete listing of different procedures required of all classrooms can be found in *My Classroom Management Book*, 2nd edition (Wong & Wong, 2018). Not only does it identify the procedures you need to address, but it is also filled with a multitude of strategies for implementation of these procedures.

Wong and Wong (2018b) make perfectly clear, that a classroom procedure is not a rule. It is a routine of the classroom. Specifically, Wong and Wong (2018b) state "RULES dictate how students BEHAVE; PROCEDURES deter-

Essential Elements for Developing Procedures and Routines in the Classroom.

1. Develop a list of all activities that you will need to establish a procedure or routine for in the classroom.
2. Generate a "step-by-step" list of how you want the students to follow the particular procedure.
3. Model the procedure for the students.
4. Select several students to model the procedure, offering feedback.
5. Take time to practice and reinforce these new procedures for the students during your first two weeks of school so that routines are established.

mine how things ARE DONE" (p. 141). You need to revamp or add new procedures as the year progresses. Your procedures and rules "set the climate—the social environment" of your classroom. As Evertson and Emmer (2013) interject, "... the established rules and procedures must be taught, practiced, and consistently reinforced" (p. 44).

HOW DO CLASSROOM JOBS AID IN THE DEVELOPMENT IN A CLASSROOM COMMUNITY?

To build a sense of community in the classroom, you first must be able to build relationships with your students. Teacher Preparation Programs cannot teach you how to relate to children; You should constantly reflect and ask yourself, "How will I build relationships and relate to my students?" (Haberman, 1995, 2005; Hill-Jackson & Stafford, 2017). I used humor, sports, and an open, authentic personality with my students; I shared my life with them, as well, and felt quite comfortable doing so. You need to determine your personal comfort level.

I learned in my first year of teaching that I was spending too much of my instructional time dealing with issues of classroom management and discipline; I was spending time in the hallway with students trying to mediate conflicts. At the end of the day, I was picking up trash, organizing the desks, to name a few. I wanted to give these tasks to my students so that they could take ownership of the classroom; I wanted my classroom at the end of the day to look as if it was the beginning of the day. Thus was the beginning of the classroom jobs. I made a list of classroom jobs that I believed that the students could complete and would result in a well-organized classroom. Typical jobs as the line leader, door greeter, fire marshal, errand runner, private secretaries, and librarians were presented to the class. I provided a list of jobs so that each student had the opportunity to hold at least one means of employment. (A complete list of jobs is provided in the Appendix, which could easily be changed to meet the needs of your classroom). Students had a complete a job application (Also included in the Appendix), for the job they were interested it, complete with references. For example, one job was a Trash Officer whose job was to give tickets to students who left trash around their desks after the set time to clean up their area. I also had a Desk Officer, who too, gave tickets for having a messy desk. These tickets had to be paid with their Mc-Bucks before they could shop at our Classroom Store. Often, new jobs emerged when unanticipated happenings occurred in the classroom.

When students performed their job poorly, they could get fired, and I would announce a new job opening to the class. The "fired" student learned valuable lessons of life:

1. They were not holding up to the responsibilities of their job.
2. They could not pay their bills or shop at our Classroom Store.

Needless to say, they were anxious to find and apply for a new job and waited impatiently for a new job to be announced.

Building a classroom community did not just involve the assignment of jobs to the students. As a teacher, I believed in this notion of community since most of my students had no idea what a working community entailed. My actions and beliefs had to be expressed to my students (Hardin, 2008). I valued the unique talents the students brought to the classroom. As Haberman (1995, 2005) advocates, I knew my class as individual students-their likes and dislikes and their strengths and weaknesses, and they knew mine. I thrived to build upon each. We discussed common threads in their and my life—how we were alike and different, and how our perspectives were

> During my time as a student, I was taught community, time management, and how to save and invest. This was a valuable foundation as I conditioned to advance in school. The McBuck System also taught me the importance of saving money.
> Jimmy Clouse, Former Student

TABLE 2.1. Building Community in the Classroom

Step-by-Step Building Community in the Classroom

Reflect on your personal interactions with your students. Do you have personal/professional relations with your students? Do you know their likes and dislikes? Do they know yours? Do you notice simple things, like a new haircut or outfit?

Use problem solving or peer mediation to develop solutions to classroom disturbances, instead of just handing out punishments. This was the purpose of our Classroom Court Model.

Are you aware of those students who are struggling or having difficulty with the curriculum? Can you produce at least 6 strategies to help them? Do you delve into what the students know, and build up from there?

Reduce the number of extrinsic rewards. I used our classroom money, McBucks, as students had to earn the for a job well done. After they earned their money, they could spend it at our Classroom store. This reduced tremendously on the amount of money I was spending on special prizes and treats.

If students are off task, there is no need to call them out. Simply walking near them will bring them back on task. I learned a valuable lesson from my first principle; I no longer called on students with their hands up. I would call on any student, and say, "Barry, what do you think about that?" Barry could respond by saying "I need more think time" or "I'd like to phone a friend, in which they could call on a friend who would give them tips and clues for the answer. This helped everyone stay on task because they never knew when I would call on them.

Assist students in building relations and friendships with their peers. Point out the many things they have in common.

Take on community projects as a class. We were pen pals with a World War II veteran, who wrote us letters about his experiences during the war. With the advancement of technology, you could connect to different classrooms world-wide.

Show the sane courtesy to your students that you expect to show you. Smiles often and avoid all means when it comes to embarrassing your students.

> Right from the first day of school, we create a culture of family. We take care of each other—we are all friends.
> Kathy Armstrong Wise, Teacher

developed and shaped (Hardin, 2008). Most importantly, our classroom was a place where they could share their talents, and where they were free to share these skills for the good of the community (Hardin, 2008). Harden (2008 p. 141) does best in describing the steps in building community in the classroom.

CLASSROOM MONEY: MCBUCKS

> I think of your McBucks economy. I contribute it to Eric being a CPA and having a double master's degree in Business and Finance. You never know how far your influence goes!
> Heather Jankovich, Parent

I knew that in my attempt to create this mini-society, I had to emulate the real world and assist my students in understanding how the world works: when individuals had a job, they expected to be paid. Thus, came the creation of our classroom money: McBucks. You can use any name for your money, but I called mine by playing off my last name. I simply designed my money as $1, $5, $10, $20- and $50-dollar bills. Every two weeks the students would get paid. This task was the responsibility of the Payroll Department. They had a list of each students' job(s) and would put the students earned McBucks in a personal envelope and deliver their pay. Students could get fired for not "showing up" or completing their job up to the standards set. Students could also receive a bonus in their pay for performing their job beyond standards and expectations. I created a "Bonus Letter" that recognized their superior job performance, and gave these letters to the Payroll Department, who would include these bonuses within their pay. I want to emphasize that this procedure was the responsibility of the Payroll Department (classroom job) and required little of my professional and instructional time. I then had to construct meaningful usage and value to their earned McBucks and extend the student's motivation to earn our classroom money. I opened a Classroom Store that sold candy, school supplies, chips—many of which were donated by my parents, neighbors, and the community. Students could also "buy" computer time and library time when classroom assignments were completed. This can easily be extended to purchase other privileges, such as Lunch with the Teacher.

> I still remember the name of my community…Grapevine-because "I Heard It Through the Grapevine" was my favorite song. We solved all our discipline issues in the classroom. My classmates were rarely sent to the principal's office. We all grew up to be productive citizens with good jobs. Even after 30+ years, our friendship bonds still exist.
> Jamal Johnson, Former Student

This is a perfect opportunity for teachers and students to identify creative ways for the use of their McBucks. Students in my class could purchase their desks and start their own community. When lottery tickets became legal in the state of Virginia, my students used their creativity and developed a system that we could sell lottery tickets in our classroom store. If you had a winning lottery ticket, you could be rewarded with additional McBucks or Homework Passes. They created a game ticket called "Lucky 21." The student creators put mathematics problems that had to be solved to determine if you had a winning ticket. If your answer to a mathematical problem was 21, you had a winning ticket and would receive $21 McBucks. I also used McBucks as a motivational tool. When we played classroom games or I recognized exceptional student behavior, they could earn McBucks. We even had a classroom bank, McKinney's Savings and Loans where students could save their money, and make withdrawals, if necessary.

Holidays can be especially hard on many students in poverty. They have limited, if any, opportunities, or resources to afford or purchase gifts for their family and loved ones. Here is where the McBucks played another role. Again, seeking donations from the community, family, and friends, we held a classroom auction where students could purchase gifts for their family, complete with wrapping paper and bows. This contributed to their drive to earn McBucks; they were learning latent talents such as creativity, determination and commitment-talents that would serve them well later in life. Therefore, the McBucks served as both an extrinsic (you want to earn a reward) and intrinsic (personally rewarding; personally, knowing a job was well done) motivational tool. Figure 2.1 shows the connections.

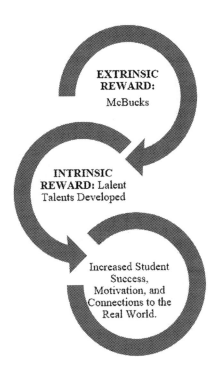

FIGURE 2.1. Extrinsic and Intrinsic Motivation

I'LL SEE YOU IN COURT: A MODEL FOR CONFLICT RESOLUTION, PEER MEDIATION, AND SELF-DISCIPLINE

The goal of a teacher is partly to create autonomous and self-directed students. This includes teaching students how to manage and solve conflicts. Students who can solve their own problems amongst themselves show maturity and responsibility that become dispositions for success later in life. According to Warters (2022), "School-based peer mediation is one of the most popular and effective approaches to integrating the practice of conflict resolution into schools. From the start of the modern "conflict resolution in education" (CRE) movement in the early 1980s, peer mediation has been one of its centerpieces. Many thousands of schools in the US and in dozens of other countries have implemented peer mediation programs, and these efforts serve almost every conceivable student population" (para. 1). A more recent acronym is CRPM for conflict resolution/peer mediation.

What is Peer Mediation? According to Isenberg (2019), "Peer mediation is a process where trained students function as neutral mediators. These students collaborate with their peers to uncover the root causes of their disputes and decide on fairways of resolving a conflict. The process is great because it's a form of restorative discipline, and helps students build their empathy while they also fine-tune their problem-solving skills" (para. 1). This switches the school's focus from punishment to conflict resolution. The steps of Peer Mediation are:

1. Parties agree to mediate
2. Parties tell their stories
3. Parties focus on interests and needs
4. Mediators work on creating win-win situations
5. Parties evaluate options
6. Parties create an agreement (Isenberg, 2019, para. 4).

Sandwick et al. (2019) say that behind conflict resolution is social and restorative justice. They posit that "restorative justice techniques interrupt the "school-to-prison pipeline," which disproportionately impacts students by race, sexuality, and disability. A small but growing research literature suggests that restorative justice decreases suspension and behavioral incidents, while improving school climate—particularly when embraced as a schoolwide ethos, rather than a targeted disciplinary strategy. Restorative justice represents a marked departure from long-standing punitive approaches to discipline, however, and school communities are eager for support in navigating this culture shift" (p. 1). Sandwick et al. (2019) mention the rise in restorative justice programs in schools across America that respond to bullying and violence at school. It has become policy in some school districts, such as in New York City as of 2019.

DOES PEER MEDIATION REALLY WORK?

The promise of successful peer mediation in resolving conflicts is unbounded. Imagine if students could use conflict resolution to avoid potential school shootings that are so ubiquitous in America today? Of course, even the best peer mediation is not enough to completely resolve the problem of school violence, especially those that are the result of mental illness, but they would go a long way. Turnuklu et al. (2009) state: "Probably the most popular conflict resolution training program in schools today is peer mediation which is basically a structured process in which a neutral and impartial student assists two or more students to negotiate an integrative resolution to their conflict (Johnson et al., 1995). Mediation is also described as a process which involves disputants actively in the resolution of their own conflicts, assisted by trained peers (Telson & McDonald,1992). Johnson and Johnson (1996, b) conclude that peer mediation programs reduce the rates of suspensions and detentions, referrals to the principal, and absenteeism, while increasing students' self-confidence, academic time on task, and academic achievement" (p. 631). Turnuklu et al. (2009) also found from studies they ran over the course of two years in high schools in Turkey that "…it is possible to conclude that CRPM programs can prove to be an effective alternative in preventing school violence and building a more peaceful society both in western and other cultures"(p. 637).

Sandwick et al., (2019) cited research that suggested that schools engaged in restorative justice practices experienced decreases in behavioral incidents and use of suspensions…and that restorative justice contributes to meaningful changes in both school culture and disciplinary responses; fosters communication and accountability, and promotes empathy, social-emotional learning, and conflict resolution (Sadwick et al., 2019, p. 5).

My mother worked for the Police Department in my city, and her responsibility was typing up any warrant proposed. She assisted me with the creation of a Classroom Warrant that was elementary student friendly yet contained the indispensable features of an actual warrant. A copy of our Classroom Warrant is provided in the Appendix.

THE TRANSITION TO CLASSROOM COURT

Although Classroom Court is a model to support peer mediation and conflict resolution, as well as self-discipline, the mini society in which Classroom Court is a function of, supports many ideals of different behavioral theories. For example, it addresses different elements of the Behavioral Approach to classroom management such as our rules and consequences, not getting "fired" from their job for inferior performance and earning McBucks. It also supports elements of Assertive Discipline by allowing the rights of the students to be met and the determining the verdict and appropriate consequences and punishment of the judge when found guilty. Further, it serves as a model of Judicious Discipline, in which students are treated and provided with justice, freedom, and equality, and that their rights are protected (Hardin, 2008).

As you will read further, all students attended "Law School" to understand the judiciary system of solving problems, the vocabulary used in such a system, and the proceedings of a trial.

Our classroom was transformed into a courtroom by moving desks around to create the Judges Bench, (The judges' wardrobe consisted of wearing my old college graduation gown, and my principal, Ms. Brinkley donated a gavel for us to use), where the jury would sit, and were the lawyers and those under question would testify. As mentioned earlier, a bailiff and magistrate were two of our classroom jobs. The bailiff was responsible for keeping order in our classroom court; the magistrate oversaw the classroom warrants, including the management of McBucks for taking out a warrant, (I charged 50 McBucks), and keeping them in order based on the date submitted. He was also charged with assisting me in setting the docket each week. My first year of implementation, all students wanted to go to court so they were taking warrants out on each other for trivial or non-essential reasons. That's when I moved to charging McBucks to take out a warrant, a procedure that actually occurs in our judicial system. This forced the students to think critically about whether the offense was troubling enough to cost them 50 McBucks. A copy of the Classroom Docket is provided in the Appendix.

When students felt that another peer has violated their rights, they no longer needed to respond with aggressive behavior or cause a major disruption in the classroom. "I'll See You in Court" became the phrase in response to classroom behavioral situations.

UNFORESEEN HAPPENINGS AND EVENTS

As in the real world, many unforeseen happenings, and events occurred each year I implement this mini-society and Classroom Court. Let me start with the positive. I saw and experienced students learning the concepts of developing into a responsible peer. This was evidenced through their job performances and the pride that developed within a job well done. Latent talents, such as leadership, creativity, "thinking outside the box," and dependability were readily displayed using this model, which could have gone unnoticed. For example, when I started this model and was setting the docket each Monday, all students volunteered to serve as lawyers for each other. After a few months of implementation of Classroom Court, one girl, (Tamara-Pseudonym) was selected to serve as the defense attorney for her peer, who was accused of pulling another girl's hair and attempting to start a fight. The defense attorney put a witness on the stand (Katina-Pseudonym) who stated she saw the whole event, and yes, that student did try to start a fight. When it was time for Tamara to question the witness, she asked to use my attendance book to show that Katina could not have witnessed the event because she was absent that day. From that day forward, Tamara started charging McBucks for her lawyer services. That situation led to discussions about lying under oath and the importance of telling the truth. We further talked about how any witness or complainant that displayed lying under oath, could truly impact a case and could cause an innocent person to be found guilty, and vice versa.

Tamara served as the model who displayed standards for the other students who wanted to serve as lawyers. Other teachers were often called as witnesses if they saw a behavioral situation involving my students. I fondly remember a case that one student brought to court. He accused another student of hitting him. The student serving as the defense attorney called our School Nurse to serve as a witness and asked her if the complainant needed medical attention on the identified date.

> I actually became an entrepreneur in 5th grade! Me and my friends started a cleaning business in which our peers would pay us McBucks to clean out their desks so they wouldn't get a ticket for having a messy desk. This was the foundation that served as my entrepreneurship journey. I am now the owner of three successful businesses: TRS Productions, TRS KIDS, and MELIQ on the Move.
>
> Tonya Rollins-Shadley, Former Student

Students asked if they could open and operate their own businesses and charge McBucks for their services. Of course, I agreed, and looked forward to seeing how this would emerge. Students opened their own Law Offices, Desk Cleaning Businesses, and Art Services became part of our society, an early beginning to entrepreneurships. They made posters which they proudly taped to the front of their desks, advertising their place of business.

We also experienced some unfortunate events, as well. Raphael (Pseudonym) tried to bribe the jury by offering to give them a quarter if they found him innocent. Tampering with the jury is a real-life situation that happens, even today. This led to many discussions of past cases involving jury tampering throughout history. I learned from this situation that I would not announce the jury until the day of court, and we remedied the situation by selecting a jury from another class.

CHAPTER 3

LAW SCHOOL

William McConnell

What does Law School entail? How can learning terms that focus on court assist with student's communication skills? Will it also assist in other ways for the students?

To begin the process of implementation of a judiciary system, or 'Classroom Court' as a means of self-discipline and classroom mediation, we studied the legal system at an elementary and/or middle school level. If I sincerely wanted this classroom management and discipline system to be successful, I first had to gain a detailed understanding of the judicial system myself because I only held general knowledge. As Haberman (2005) would say, "You can't teach what you don't know!" I began the process with the students by having them view countless clips of "Matlock, Perry Mayson, and Court T.V. The students were given specific tasks to complete as we viewed these clips and held discussions during instruction. A few specific tasks and discussions/instruction included:

1. How is a court room designed and where so some of the involved participants sit?
2. What were some of the people's roles and responsibilities you noted?
3. What were the common procedures and steps that were followed in the trial process?

4. Why was there an oath that the participants had to swear to?
5. What instructions were given to the jury, and how were they selected?
6. How did a jury reach a decision?
7. Who decides the sentence and how was it imposed?
8. What common terms were being used, and when would they be used?

TEACHING STUDENTS TO CRITICALLY THINK LIKE A LAWYER

Often, many teachers view and believe that only advanced or upper-level students can deal with and develop the skills necessary skills for application (Seale, 2020). Seale (2020) advocated this belief by stating the response of one student to his question, "What is critical thinking? This student response speaks volumes: "Critical thinking is what teachers never let us do in school" (p. 15). Some teachers believe that critical thinking involves just asking higher level questions based on Bloom's Taxonomy (1956) which include Knowledge, Comprehension, Application, Analysis, Syntheses, and Evaluation. Over the years, the taxonomy has been updated by cognitive psychologists, curriculum theorists, researchers, and testing and assessment specialists and are presented in *A Taxonomy for Learning and Assessing: A Revision of Blooms Taxonomy of Educational Objectives (Anderson & Krathwohl,* 2001). They describe and expand the cognitive processes used by critical thinkers using action terms. A summary of these processes is identified in Table 3.1.

> Being a lawyer in my 5th grade class made me feel smart and needed. I couldn't let my client down. I was in competition with the other lawyer. I was put in a role that required authority. The research required for preparing my case was demanding I had to conduct numerous interviews to determine what really happened, and how to get the jury to understand the points I was making. All eyes were on me in this role.
> — Antonio Yancey, Former Student

Seale (2020) also argues that critical thinking involves student dispositions, as well. These dispositions include Inquisitiveness, Truth-Seeking, Self-Confidence, and Maturity. Our next step was moving on to learning and understanding the

TABLE 3.1. A Revision of Bloom's Taxonomy

Categories	Subcategories
Remember	Recognizing, Recalling
Understand	Interpreting, Exemplifying, Classifying, Summarizing, Inferring, Comparing, Explaining
Apply	Executing, Implementing
Analyze	Differentiating, Organizing, Attributing
Evaluate	Checking, Critiquing
Create	Generating, Planning, Producing

(Anderson & Krathwohl, 2001)

legal language used in a court room and being able to apply it correctly in different situations.

At least one law critic has suggested that the high level of complexity and technicality of today's legal terms is a ploy to increase the income of lawyers and judges and/or to confuse the public (Postema, 1986). Whether you agree with this opinion or not, it is certainly arguable that most adults have trouble understanding common legal language. If you have signed legal documents or been to court, it is likely that you are familiar with the feeling of confusion when encountering legalese in a document, or worse, in verbal form. How could we have been more prepared for this legal vocabulary?

In elementary school, students may learn a scant number of terms related to colonial governments. In middle school, students may learn about a case or two, and the three major branches of government, but many of the legal terms that are used in court or in congress fail to make it into the curriculum. Then, in high school, government teachers address the broad practices of political science in America, again, mostly without addressing the common language that happens in trials, on legal forms, or even the legal vocabulary a young adult may hear when receiving their first traffic ticket. Further, the small amount of important legal vocabulary that is learned in school is often through rote memorization, with seemingly little to no relevance to most students' lives. Thus, students are not using the vocabulary purposely in class or outside of class and their retention of these terms is most often only short-term. Studies suggest that even students in primary grades can learn complex vocabulary through explicit instruction (Hanson & Padua, 2011). Explicit instruction of vocabulary requires the teacher to introduce the term using developmentally appropriate language, involve ample opportunities for practice through different modalities (e.g., written, drawing, and oral discussion), and provide meaningful opportunities for students to use the words in context.

DEVELOPMENTALLY APPROPRIATE LANGUAGE

In Table 3.2 we modified a list of legal terms from *Legal Words You Should Know* (Sandler & Keefe, 2009) to make them more elementary-appropriate. When introducing these terms, it is also important to provide realistic examples related to your students' lives. One common scenario is the case of spilled milk. It may be easier for your students to understand the term "Confession" when they relate it to when someone states, "I spilled the milk."

PRACTICE THROUGH DIFFERENT MODALITIES

There are many ways to have your students practice the terms in different modalities. For elementary students, it may be beneficial to begin a Legal Word Wall that you can add on throughout the year and students can add to their notebooks. Having students illustrate the meaning of the word near its posting can also assist in learning of all students, including those learning English as a second language

TABLE 3.2. Legal Terms and Developmentally Appropriate Definitions

Term/Phrase	Elementary Description
Abuse	(1). When students feel that they have been mistreated (e.g., emotionally, physically) or have been treated unkindly or cruelly by another. (2). The inappropriate use of a right or privilege.
Accommodation	When students assist another student, such as a favor, without expecting a reward or payment of classroom money (McBucks).
Accomplice	A student who aids in the mission of mistreating another student or participating in a classroom crime (e.g., stealing).
Accuse	To be charged with a crime or unfair treatment of another.
Acquit	The defendant is found not guilty of the charge made against him/her.
Adjournment	Postponing a court session.
Admissible	When students are allowed to use any evidence or testimony during their court case.
Alibi	The student was elsewhere when the crime was committed.
Allegation	To state a fact or an action.
Accessory	Assisted with the commission of a crime without direct participation.
Attorney-Client Privilege	Protection of communication between lawyer and client.
Beyond a Reasonable Doubt	An exceedingly high standard of proof.
Bribery	An attempt to influence a student's behavior by giving them something of value.
Case	A case is when all of us hear all sides of the story about a specific event and then we decide what to do.
Chain of Custody	This is a list of people who have had something important.
Character Witness	This is someone who knows you well and can tell others how you usually act or behave.
Charge	A charge is when someone says that someone else did something wrong.
Circumstantial Evidence	Evidence that may be important, but it doesn't prove anyone's guilt in the matter.
Citation	A notice to appear in court for some sort of crime.
Clear and Convincing Evidence	This is when evidence is clear and strong enough to prove something in court.
Closing Statement	The final summary for each side of a case.
Complaint	A formal complaint made to seek some sort of action from the court.
Confession	When someone states that they did something wrong.
Conspiracy	A secret agreement between two or more people to break a rule or law or to get away with something.
Contempt	This is a formal finding from the judge or court officers that someone has been disrespectful or is purposely not following court rules.

TABLE 3.2. Continued

Term/Phrase	Elementary Description
Conviction	When the judge or jury finds someone guilty of a crime.
Court Order	When the court or judge requires something of someone or a group.
Cross Examine	When a witness for one side of an argument is questioned by the other side.
Decision	At the end of a trial, the ruling of the judge or jury.
Defamation	When someone says something untrue on purpose just to make someone else look bad.
Defendant	The person in a trial that is accused of a crime.
Deposition	This is a recording of testimony from a witness before a trial.
Disclose	To reveal a secret.
Discrimination	Treating one person or small group of people differently or unfairly.
Direct Examination	When the person who called a witness questions them.
Due Process	This is the promise that everyone will be treated fairly in a trial.
Emotional Distress	When someone requests some sort of payout from another person or group who has done something against them.
Equity	Fairness or equality in court.
Expert Witness	A person that has no relation to the trial but has great knowledge about a specific matter and can help the court better understand an event or topic.
Extortion	When someone or a group threatens someone or a group to get something they want.
Eyewitness	Someone who saw an event happen related to the trial and presents what happened to the court.
Fault	One who is responsible for a problem, an act, or accident.
Fine	A penalty that demands a payment of money.
Forge	To create a fake or partly fake formal document to deceive someone.
Fraud	To purposefully trick or lie to someone to get something that you want.
Harassment	Repeated, unwanted acts that annoy or upset someone.
Hearsay	When someone tells the court what they heard someone else say. This is usually not allowed in court.
Hung Jury	When the jury cannot agree on a decision related to who will win the trial.
Immaterial	Evidence that does not relate to the issue in the case.
Inadmissible	When the court will not allow a piece of evidence to be shared in trial for any reason.
Incite	An act or words that encourage others to feel a certain way.
Injury	Any harm done to someone—physical or otherwise.
Interrogation	Questioning of someone by authorities.

(continues)

TABLE 3.2. Continued

Term/Phrase	Elementary Description
Jury	A group of people who are gathered to hear a case and decide on the guilt of a person.
Lawsuit	When one person or group has a case against another person or group because they feel they have been wronged in some way.
Liability	Responsibility for your acts or lack of action.
Mandatory	Required by law or rules.
Material Witness	Someone who has information that is important to the issue to share in a trial.
Mistrial	When a trial ends before a decision because of an issue in the procedure.
Negotiable	A topic that can be discussed and agreed upon for both sides.
Not Guilty	When a jury or judge does not find that there is enough evidence to find someone guilty.
Objection	An attorney's argument that someone is not following trial procedures.
Opening Statement	The first statement of an attorney just before a trial that outlines their story, or case.
Overrule	When the judge rejects, or doesn't agree with, an objection in a trial.
Pain and Suffering	Physical or mental pain caused by someone else.
Perjury	When someone purposely lies in court.
Prejudice	When someone finds fault in an individual without evidence and only due to bias.
Preponderance of Evidence	When the strength of evidence is enough to convince someone.
Prevail	To win a court proceeding.
Proof	When evidence establishes fact in a case.
Prosecution	The authorities' side in a case.
Punitive Damage	Money or something to be paid as punishment from those found guilty to the winner in a case.
Reasonable Doubt	When all evidence is presented, and the jury still is not sure that the person is guilty.
Ruling	A decision made by the judge.
Settlement	A solution between two parties outside of court.
Slander	When someone says something to make someone look or seem bad.
Sue	To begin a lawsuit against someone or a group.
Summation	The final summary from an attorney to the judge or jury that sums up all evidence and asks for a decision in their favor.
Sustain	When the court agrees to an objection.
Testimony	Someone's formal statements in court.
Verdict	A jury's final decision.
Warrant	An order from the court allowing authorities to search someone's things or make an arrest.
Wrongful	Something that is against the rules or unfair.

(Gallagher & Anderson, 2016). Students can also write and/or draw the meaning of the terms in their notebooks. With a word wall, the teacher can easily review and refer to the wall throughout the year.

MEANINGFUL USE OF TERMS

This book provides a unique and meaningful context that can assist teachers in effectively teaching many legal terms to their students. When using the strategies in the text, students should be encouraged to reference the word wall or their notebooks and to use appropriate legal terms. By the end of the year, your students will have had ample practice using these terms in authentic contexts. I am including the legal vocabulary I used for my elementary school students.

LEGAL TERMS STUDENTS SHOULD KNOW, UNDERSTAND, AND BE ABLE TO APPLY

One year we were granted special permission to participate in a field trip to Norfolk District Court to view a local trial. Normally, only the upper middle school participate in this type of trip. During the jury deliberations of the actual trial, the judge allowed my students to ask him any questions. I sat there a bit anxious, having no idea or clue what type of questions they would ask. My students presented their questions and made comments to the judge; I sat there beaming, feeling like the greatest teacher in the world. Not only were their questions of higher level, but they were also critically analyzing and synthesizing the case. They demonstrated skills of thinking like a lawyer and started to involve the prosecuting and defense attorneys with their questions and comments. The Judge even allowed several of my students to sit on the Judge's bench. Upon dismissal, I commented to the Judge that he was going to see my students in court one day in some type of professional judicial role.

CHAPTER 4

COURT DOCKET AND JURY SELECTION

How is the court docket set and organized? Which cases are heard each week? How is the jury selected? Do they always make the right decision?

"Members of the Jury, you will rise, hold up your right hands, and be sworn to try this case." The jurors then rise and hold up their right hands. The jurors face the judge or the clerk who is to administer the oath. That official slowly, solemnly, and clearly repeats the oath. The jurors indicate by their responses and upraised hands that they take this solemn oath. Jurors not wishing to take an oath may request to affirm instead of swearing. In some districts the jury is sworn upon the Bible and not by uplifted hand.

WHAT IS THE PURPOSE OF A DOCKET?

A docket is defined by the Administrative Office of the U.S. Courts as a "log containing the complete history of each case in the form of brief chronological entries summarizing the court proceedings" (Library of Congress, 2022). Our court docket was announced every Monday; the magistrate (classroom job) was tasked with organizing the warrants (cases) based on the date submitted. I would announce the case, and charges brought against the defendant, and the plaintiff and defendant would select their lawyers. Once a lawyer proved his/her expertise in the courtroom, they started charging McBucks. Any witnesses or others that could contribute to the case were also announced. The plaintiff would also indicate what they were suing for (Punishment).

I used to announce the jury on Monday as well. That is until one student tried to bribe the jury by offering them a quarter if they found him innocent. After that incident, jury members were not announced until right before the court case; "The primary purpose of the jury is to prevent oppression by the government and provide the accused a "safeguard against the corrupt or overzealous prosecutor and against the complaint, biased, or eccentric judge" (Neubauer & Fradella, 2017, p. 354). A sample docket is provided in the Appendix.

THE NATURE AND IMPORTANCE OF THE ROLE OF JURORS

> Serving on the jury forced me to think critically, problem solve, and review the evidence to determine the guilt or innocence of the defendant (my peers). I learned to "think outside the box." These principles still guide my thinking today.
> Candace Jones, Former Student

Jury members are charged with performing an essential public service to our Classroom Court Model. Students took turns acting as the Judge, and the Judge would instruct the jury of the pending case. For example, the Judge will inform the jury that a defendant is presumed innocent and the burden of proving guilt or innocence lies within them. Collaboratory, the Judge and jury protect our rights, liberties, and freedom. The students serving on the jury must be of sound judgement, honesty, and fairness. This leaves the students with a feeling that they performed their duty honorably, in the pursuit of life, liberty, and the pursuit of happiness. They are sworn to discount their personal prejudices and biases so that they may render a decision, or verdict, based on an open mind to make the best judgement according to their abilities (Administrative Office of the US Courts, 2022).

During jury selection, the attorneys of each party have the right to dismiss a potential based on any bias, the leading being close friendships. Once the 12 jury members are selected, the judge communicates the jury oath, and the court case then proceeds.

The critical thinking and problem required of the jury is complex and requires a ." . . critical disposition of inquisitiveness: the habit of probing beyond the surface." (Seale, 2020, p. 44). They must determine if they believe the defendant of plaintiff, which witness they believe, and they must also weigh the evidence. Collectively, they must analyze the case from multiple perspectives, and converse persuasively with their peers (Seale, 2020). They are then required to draw a conclusion based on the analysis of the evidence—guilty or innocent.

Borrowing from Seale (2020), I developed a rubric that would assist the jury with deciding the case.

TABLE 4.1. Guidelines to Assist Jury Members

Guidelines to Assist with Jury Decision:	
What is the case being presented?	
Plaintiff and Prosecuting Attorney	**Defendant and Defense Attorney**
The Plaintiff Attorney clearly stated the foundation of the case; articulated how his/her client was treated unfairly; how this treatment affected their client, and how the defendant could disrupt the community built within the classroom.	The Defense Attorney clearly stated how his/her client is innocent. Provides a persuasive argument to support this claim.
Provides evidence, facts, and witnesses to support the case, with a persuasive argument for each.	Discounts the evidence, facts, and witnesses with a persuasive argument. Has conflicting evidence and witnesses.
Summarizes the case with the evidence presented with key arguments.	Discounts the evidence with a strategic argument.
Verdict:	

I wish I could say my students made the correct decision for each case, though they did get stronger with their decision-making process as the year progressed. I distinctly remember our first court case. The plaintiff submitted a warrant, accusing another student of disturbing the learning environment by singing in class. Because the plaintiff could not name the song the defendant was singing, she was found innocent. Unmistakably, I had a long road to travel in teaching my students critical thinking and problem-solving skills. However, we did discuss if the title of the song was relevant in determining if the student was singing during class time. After a class discussion, with both sides being argued by students, they finally agreed that it was not, and so the process of thinking critical thinking from multiple perspectives began.

What would schools think of this management and discipline system today? Interestingly, Haberman (2005) states that school reformers, especially for urban schools, intermittently attempt to move beyond the basic skill level, to focus on such topics of critical thinking, solving problems, and even latent talents like creativity. Further he believes that until the "Pedagogy of Poverty" is addressed, legitimate and genuine thinking will not be obliged. Haberman refers to the "Pedagogy of Poverty" as a body of teaching acts (e.g., giving directions, making assignments, asking questions, punishing non-compliance, and giving grades) That becomes routines of the classroom. Other scholars also support the inequalities of teaching through the lens of poverty (Hoadley, 2018; Ladson-Billings, 2014)

Haberman (2005) best describes Real or Good Teaching as:

1. "Whenever students are involved with issues they regard as vital concerns, good teaching is going on" (p. 54).
2. Whenever students are involved with explanations of human differences, good teaching is going on" (p. 55).
3. Whenever students are being helped to see major concepts, big ideas, and general principles and not merely engaged in the pursuit of isolated facts, good teaching is going on" (p. 55).
4. Whenever students are involved in planning and what they will be doing, it is likely good teaching is going on" (p.55).
5. When students are involved with applying ideals such as fairness, equality, or justice in their world, it is likely that good teaching is going on" (p. 55).
6. Whenever students are directly involved in a real-life experience, it is likely that good teaching is going on (p. 55).

According to Haberman's ideology, (1995, 2005, 2012, 2017), we believe this Classroom Court Model is an example of "Good teaching going on." I believe my students would agree.

CHAPTER 5

SENTENCING

Who was responsible for sentencing the student if they were found guilty? What are some sentences, or "consequences" the student could face in court? What factors about urban learners should be taken into consideration?

As I begin the sentencing procedures and practices we followed in our "Classroom Court," I always share a story about me as a second-grade student. It had such an impact on me, that I even share it with my preservice teachers that I work with now at the university (With my wit and humor, I let my preservice teachers know that with extensive therapy over the years, I have fully recovered from the situation).

I can remember this situation as if it happened yesterday, instead of over 50 years ago. I was a student that found learning extremely easy for me in second grade, and when I would finish my work, I would take it upon myself to get up out of my seat and help my peers who were struggling. I guess at an incredibly early age my DNA knew I was going to be a teacher! I never felt like I was breaking a classroom rule, and my talking with my peer was always about explaining the content. The teacher would always discipline me—but I never understood what I was doing wrong. Looking back, I suspect she was a novice teacher, early in her career, and struggled with classroom management and discipline, although I don't recall it being an "out of control" classroom. One day, my teacher walked in and stated, "If we were going to act like babies, she was going to treat us like babies,"

> The role of an urban teacher is to educate and care. Students may not have much of a light in their own lives, especially those in urban communities. School is not only a place to learn and develop oneself, but it is also to find a light in life. People grasp onto what is good and a teacher who has a profound, uplifting, and compassionate demeanor will create years of an impact on a child. That is the good, the light, the students, and the world of education needs.
> — Savannah Coons, Teacher

and proceeded to put a baby mat on the floor in front of the class. She informed us that if we were caught being bad, we would have to go and lay on the baby mat in front of everyone. Guess who had to lay on that baby mat first.

I had on a blue "sailor like" dress with red trim. My socks were the rolled down type with lace, popular in the late 60s, and I was wearing patent leather shoes. I lay on the mat, facing the wall, embarrassed that the boys could look up my dress. I was humiliated and cried extensively while I laid there. From that moment on, I hated my teacher. I no longer participated in class, helped my peers, or volunteered for any activity. She killed my spirit for learning that day in second grade, and I have never forgotten that feeling.

I share this story with you for two reasons. Embarrassing a student should never be used as a form of punishment or discipline. Moreover, how we discipline is just as significant; my teacher destroyed my spirit to learn. Our behavior as teachers may have unanticipated and unseen consequences for a student's self-worth and esteem. I made a promise each year to my class that I would never humiliate them through discipline.

SENTENCING GUIDELINES

When it came to sentencing the student that was found guilty by his/her peers in our "Court of Law," I would meet with the assigned Judge in the "Judges Chambers" (my desk area), and we collectively would decide the appropriate sentence for the guilty charge. We would take into consideration what the plaintiff was suing for as punishment—McBucks, time in "Chill Out," after school detention, and/or a Classroom Conduct Notice. School suspension was not an option. When we both agreed on the sentence, it was then announced in court, and the guilty student would have to serve the punishment rendered. These punishments can also be tweaked to serve the students in your present classroom. Punishments like a phone call or email to parents or sitting by themselves at lunch could also serve the purpose for your particular population of students.

THE NEED TO UNDERSTAND THE URBAN LEARNER IN ORDER TO IMPOSE THE PROPER SENTENCE

No child chooses to live and grow up in an area impacted by poverty. For the purpose of this book, we use Payne's (2019) working definition of poverty, "the extent to which an individual does without resources" (p. 7). Payne (2019) argues that there a relationship exists between the environment demands, the availability of resources, and an individual's knowledge, and is based on Bandura's study of social cognition (learning transpires when individual interrelate in different social contexts) (Navabi, 2012). This awareness can assist teachers in understanding their students in more meaningful ways a positive, interactive relationships.

> Teachers should discipline with dignity and practice cultural sensitivity. Think of your students as at-promise instead of at-risk. Set clear expectations, and avoid being rigid, and be consistent. Communicate with parents regularly and positively. If there is something you don't know, just ask.
> — Julie Perkins, Assistant Principal

Teachers must know that there are two distinct types of poverty: generational and situational. Payne (2019) defines generational poverty is when a household has been in poverty for at least two generations; situational poverty is caused by a particular situation or event (e.g., divorce, weather disasters, health), and, unlike generational poverty, can be a transitory circumstance).

Many students attending urban, high poverty schools experience generational poverty-which impacts housing stability, violence, little or lack of food, health issues, addiction, lack of personal space because of overcrowded housing, jail/prison, and uneducated or undereducated adults (Payne, 2019). This can explain many of the behaviors exhibited by the students: Laughing when disciplined, anger, arguing with authority, difficulty in following directions, and harming other students. In *A Framework for Understanding Poverty: A Cognitive Approach*, Payne provides an explanation for these behaviors as they relate to poverty, and interventions and approaches that teachers can incorporate and provide. (2019).

Haberman (1995, 2005) also explains the thought processes, behaviors, and causes of students in poverty. A few include showing up for class, a "make-me" attitude, non-cooperation, lack of respect, and messing up. He further notes that many teachers often misinterpret these behaviors and situations. Many teachers provoke these situations and behaviors because of their lack of understanding and knowledge base of living in poverty.

> I love being an urban teacher because my school is full of diversity. I also love to give back to the community I grew up in. I relate to the parents and students. I am a living example of what is possible.
> — Tasha Lemelle, Former Student and Current Teacher

As a result, they don't provide opportunities and instruction that are thought provoking, creative, and challenging.

Star Teachers are well versed in understanding the children they teach. They don't look at discipline as a "set of strategies" you implement when students misbehave. If you don't have a deep and profound relationship with each student, they will simply resort to their learned behaviors of poverty. Star teachers view discipline and consequences as norms of expected behaviors, and not just a matter between the teacher and student. Stars view discipline in the classroom in terms of justice and equity between the student offender and the class. Together, they create agreed upon benchmarks of acceptable behavior.

CHAPTER 6

THE SUPREME COURT

Starrbe Bryant

How does this model of classroom management and discipline apply to the National Standards of Learning?

The role of the Supreme Court is to ensure the American people the promise of equal justice under the law. Essentially, this is what standards of learning are intended to do for schools as well. The Standards of learning, whether national or state, are designed to ensure that teachers, students, parents, and other stakeholders have a framework of expectations for students to learn (Great Schools, 2015).

For years, American did not have National Education Standards (NES). In fact, the idea was not developed by the government, but rather by The National Council of Teachers of Mathematics (NCTM) in 1989. The NCTM published a set of standards to guide mathematics instruction. These standards were developed as a consensus amongst math experts and math teachers; the standards became a guide, or model for other content areas (Barton, 2009). Over the past two decades there has been much controversy regarding The National Standards. The intent of the standards was to design a set of standards that would raise the achievement levels of all students, decrease the increasingly widened achievement gaps, and diminish the lack of international competitiveness amongst our graduates (Barton, 2009).

According to the Great Schools Organization (2015), proponents of national standards feel that the standards would level the playing field and allow students in the US to be more competitive in the global economy, the standards would raise the expectations for all, and students who move from state to state will have a better chance of being acclimated to the coursework. Opponents proclaim that we cannot expect higher quality education just because there is more government involvement; national standards limit teacher autonomy, as it is a one-size fits all approach, and national standards discourage innovation and creativity in the classroom.

It is important to note that national standards are created by a collective body of organizations and individual states have the autonomy to adopt national standards. The state and local communities create state standards. Under Every Student Succeeds Act (ESSA), federal mandates have decreased, which has given the states more flexibility and authority, thus opening the door for more innovation and creativity (Weiss & Mcguinn, 2016).

NATIONAL STANDARDS

The National Council of Teachers of Mathematics (NCTM) provides teachers, school administration, and other stakeholders with guidance in making sound decisions that will affect students learning mathematics. There are five content standards and each of these standards incorporate specific expectations which are structured by grade level bands. The five content standards are Number & operations, Algebra, Geometry, Measurement, and Data Analysis & Probability. Additionally, there are accompanying process standards which are more elaborative, and they describe what each standard looks like and outline ways in which the teacher can achieve the intended outcome. The process standards are problem solving, reasoning and proof, communication, connections, and representation (NCTM, n.d.)

The National Council of Teachers of English (NCTE) is this nation's oldest organization of pre-k through graduate school literacy educators (NCTE, n.d.). The organization is determined to continuously improve teaching and learning in English and the language arts across all grade levels. The standards were updated in 2009 from the original iteration that was published in 1996, which were jointly created by the NCTE and The International Reading Association (IRA). The revisions focused on improving assessment by providing standards that better aligned with assessment practices of 21st-centry literacy classes. As part of their vision, the NCTE will actively pursue justice and equity for all educators and students by applying the power of language and literacy (NCTE, n.d.). The court discipline system required students to rely heavily on their communication skills to effectively defend themselves and each other. The NCTE standards address six English language arts areas: reading, writing, speaking, listening, viewing, and visually representing (NCTE, n.d.). Although the six areas may be perceived as different from one another, there are relevant connections amongst them, connections that are essential to teaching and learning the English language arts. Therefore, the NCTE and IRA suggest linking them in pairs to better see the connections.

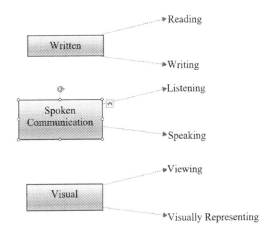

FIGURE 6.1. NCTE/IRA Language Arts Connections

WHAT'S THE CONNECTION?
CLASSROOM MONEY, COURT, AND NATIONAL STANDARDS

Creativity, innovation, and fostering critical thinking skills were some of the guiding factors for the creation of the Classroom Court System. While extrinsically and intrinsically motivating students through real world connections and practical application guided the McBucks classroom management system. Collectively, these management and discipline systems engaged learners in various national standards of learning that required students to implore critical thinking. The table below will highlight a few of the standards that were addressed in the primary focus areas of reading and math, although an in-depth study of the standards as they relate to the systems would reveal a lot more connections, based on individual perception, especially in social sciences. It is quite apparent that many of these standards are addressed through this Classroom Management and Discipline Model. Moreover, students are introduced to civics and the law at an early age.

> The "Classroom Court Model" Is a fantastic classroom behavior management tool for young adolescent students. While it might be easier for a teacher to just "call out" disruptive behavior, the Court created a culture in the classroom where students took ownership of their behavior and the subsequent consequences the Court imposed.
>
> Jeff Tayloe
> Counselor, National Board Certified

It is worthy to note that it takes a STAR teacher to step outside of the box and think of innovative ways to make learning meaningful to students while still addressing curricular standards. Haberman (1995) states, "They show how, they show interest, they involve, and they seek ways to connect subjects with the

TABLE 6.1. IRA/NCTE Standards for the English Language Arts

IRA/NCTE: National Reading Standards Addressed
Standard 1: Students read a wide range of print and nonprint texts to build an understanding of texts, of themselves, and of the cultures of the United States and the world; to acquire new information; to respond to the needs and demands of society and the workplace; and for personal fulfillment. Among these texts are fiction and nonfiction, classic and contemporary works.
Standard 3: Students apply a wide range of strategies to comprehend, interpret, evaluate, and appreciate texts. They draw on their prior experience, their interactions with other readers and writers, their knowledge of word meaning and of other texts, their word identification strategies, and their understanding of textual features (e.g., sound-letter correspondence, sentence structure, context, graphics).
Standard 4: Students adjust their use of spoken, written, and visual language (e.g., conventions, style, vocabulary) to communicate effectively with a variety of audiences and for different purposes.
Standard 7: Students conduct research on issues and interests by generating ideas and questions, and by posing problems. They gather, evaluate, and synthesize data from a variety of sources (e.g., print and nonprint texts, artifacts, people) to communicate their discoveries in ways that suit their purpose and audience.
Standard 8: Students use a variety of technological and informational resources (e.g., libraries, databases, computer networks, video) to gather and synthesize information and to create and communicate knowledge.
Standard 11: Students participate as knowledgeable, reflective, creative, and critical members of a variety of literacy communities.
Standard 12: Students use spoken, written, and visual language to accomplish their own purposes (e.g., for learning, enjoyment, persuasion, and the exchange of information).

children's background and experiences" when discussing the difference between mediocre and STAR teachers. STAR teachers can apply the standards while involving students and tapping into their interests (Haberman, 1995, 2005). Payne (2019) further explains, " Educators have tremendous opportunities to influence some of the non-financial resources that make such a difference in students' lives. For example, it costs nothing to be an appropriate role model" (p. 30).

TABLE 6.2. NCTM Standards for Mathematics

NCTM: National Math Standards Addressed
Content Standards

Number & Operations:
- Understand numbers, ways of representing numbers, relationships among numbers, and number systems.
- Understand meanings of operations and how they relate to one another.
- Compute fluently and make reasonable estimates.

Data Analysis & Probability:
- Formulate questions that can be addressed with data and collect, organize, and display relevant data to answer them.
- Select and use appropriate statistical methods to analyze data.
- Develop and evaluate inferences and predictions that are based on data.

Process Standards

Problem Solving:
- Build new mathematical knowledge through problem solving.
- Solve problems that arise in mathematics and in other contexts.
- Apply and adapt a variety of appropriate strategies to solve problems.
- Monitor and reflect on the process of mathematical problem solving.

Reasoning & Proof:
Recognize reasoning and proof as fundamental aspects of mathematics.
Make and investigate mathematical conjectures.
Develop and evaluate mathematical arguments and proofs.
Select and use various types of reasoning and methods of proof.
Develop and evaluate inferences and predictions that are based on data.

Communication:
- Recognize and use connections among mathematical ideas.
- Understand how mathematical ideas interconnect and build on one another to produce a coherent whole.
- Recognize and apply mathematics in contexts outside of mathematics.

Connections:
- Recognize and use connections among mathematical ideas.
- Understand how mathematical ideas interconnect and build on one another to produce a coherent whole.
- Recognize and apply mathematics in contexts outside of mathematics.

Representation:
- Create and use representations to organize, record, and communicate mathematical ideas.
- Select, apply, and translate among mathematical representations to solve problems.
- Use representations to model and interpret physical, social, and mathematical phenomena.

CLOSING STATEMENTS

Dear Current and Future Urban Educators:

Authoring this book about classroom management and discipline for you has brought so much joy to my professional and personal life. Reconnecting with current and former administrators, teachers, and students, some from over 35 years ago, made my heart smile. It was amazing to hear from and talk to my former students, and what they remembered about our class. I was the privileged one to be their teacher!

Divine intervention led me to teach in high-poverty schools for over 16 years. Developing teachers for this particular environment is also the leading topic of my research interest at the university. I thrive to change misperceptions and myths common to teaching in urban schools and working with children in poverty. Instead, I attempt to instill a passion and drive for educating the children who need the best teachers, the "Star Teachers" the most.

All students deserve the opportunity for equality and equity in learning situations. All students deserve to participate in their own growth and development, particularly as it pertains to problem solving and critical thinking. And all students should be involved in the management of the class, and occasions for peer mediation and self-discipline. The heart of a teacher is what drives a well-managed classroom-his/her commitment, personality, predispositions, ethics, relationships, and trust. When urban students "feel" these traits from the teacher, the classroom transforms into a magical place of learning.

As I begin to feel like the "Tom Brady of Education," and retirement approaches, my career is complete now that I have authored this book. I always wanted to share the ideals of this management and discipline approach because it worked so well. Then I talked to Ms. Brinkley, and she simply stated that someone has to continue to fight for these schools and students. With that, my journey will continue to assist in the development of "Star Teachers" so that they may change the lives of students facing poverty. Join me.

—~ Dr. Sueanne E. McKinney
Associate Professor of Urban Education

REFERENCES

Administration Office of the United States Courts. (2022). *Handbook for trial jurors serving in the United States district courts.* Thurgood Marshall Federal Judiciary Building.

Anderson, L. W., & Krathwohl, D. R. (2001). *A Taxonomy for learning, teaching and assessing: A revision of Bloom's Taxonomy of educational objectives: Complete edition.* Longman.

Barton, P. E. (2009). *National education standards—Getting beneath the surface.* Educational Testing Service.

Bloom, B. S. (1956) *Taxonomy of Educational objectives. Handbook: The cognitive domain.* David McKay.

Crawford, D. K., & Bodine, R. J. (1996). *Conflict resolution education: A guide to implementing programs in schools, youth-serving organizations, and community and juvenile justice settings.* U.S. Department of Justice, Office of Justice Programs, Office of Juvenile Justice and Delinquency Prevention, and U.S. Department of Education, Office of Elementary and Secondary Education, Safe and Drug-Free Schools Program.

Curwin, R. L., & Mendler, A. N. (1988). *Discipline with dignity.* Association for Supervision and Curriculum Development.

Del Toro, J., & Wang, M., (2021). The longitudinal inter-relations between school discipline and academic performance: Examining the role of school climate. *American Psychologist*, September 29, 2021.

Dewey, J., (1916). *Democracy and education: An introduction to the philosophy of education*. McMillan.
Evertson, C., & Emmer, E. (2013). *Classroom management for elementary teachers*. Pearson.
Gallagher, M. A., & Anderson, B. E. (2016). Get all "jazzed up" for vocabulary instruction: Strategies that engage. *The Reading Teacher, 70*(3), 273–282.
Gathercoal, F. (2001). *Judicious discipline* (6th ed.). Caddo Gap Press.
Great Schools. (2015). *Why are standards important?* Great Schools.org.
Haberman, M. (1991). The pedagogy of poverty verses good teaching. *Kappan Classic, 92*(2), 81–87.
Haberman, M. (1995). *Star teachers of children in poverty*. Routledge.
Haberman, M. (2005). *Star teachers: The ideology and best practice of effective teachers of diverse children and youth in poverty*. The Haberman Educational Foundation.
Haberman, M. (2012). *Teacher talk: When teachers face themselves*. The Haberman Educational Foundation.
Haberman, M., Gillette, M., & Hill, D. (2018). *Star teachers of children in poverty* (2nd ed.). Routledge.
Hanson, S., & Padua, J. F. (2011). *Teaching vocabulary explicitly. Effective instructional strategies series*. Pacific Resources for Education and Learning (PREL).
Hardin, C. (2008). *Effective classroom management* (2nd ed.). Pearson.
Hill-Jackson, V., & Stafford, D. (2017). *Better teachers better schools: What star teachers know, believe, and do*. Information Age Publishing.
Hoadley, U. (2018). *Pedagogy in poverty*. Routledge.
Ingersoll, R. M., & Smith, T. M. (2003). The wrong solution to the teacher shortage. *Educational Leadership, 60*, 30–33.
Isenberg, A. (2019). *What is Peer Mediation? How Does it Help Schools?* Region 13's Blog (esc13.net).
Jones, F. (1987). *Positive classroom discipline*. McGraw-Hill.
Klassen, R. M., & Chiu, M. M. (2010). Effects on teachers' self-efficacy and job satisfaction: Teacher gender, years of experience, and job stress. *Journal of Educational Psychology, 102*, 741–756. doi:10.1037/a001923
Kohlberg, L. (1958). *The development of modes of thinking and choices in years 10 to 16*. Ph. D. Dissertation, University of Chicago.
Kohlberg, L. (1984). The psychology of moral development: The nature and validity of moral stages. In *Essays on moral development (vol. 2)*. Harper & Row.
Ladson-Billings, G. (2014). Culturally relevant pedagogy 2.0: A. K. A. the remix. *Harvard Educational Review, 84*(1), 74–84. https://doi.org/10.17763/haer.84.1.p2rj131485484751
Landers, E., Alter, P., & Servilio, K. (2008). Students' challenging behavior and teachers' job satisfaction. *Beyond Behavior, 18*(1), 27–33.
Lickona, T. (1991). *Educating for character*. Bantam.
Martin, L. (2021, June). Reconceptualizing classroom management in the ensemble: Considering culture, communication, and community. *Music Educator's Journal, 70*(1), 00274321.
Myers, D., Freeman, J., Simonsen, B., & Sugai, G. (2017). Classroom management with exceptional learners. *TEACHING Exceptional Children, 49*(4), 223–230.

National Council of Teachers of Mathematics (NCTE). (n.d.). *NCTE / IRA standards for the English Language Arts*. NCTE. https://ncte.org/resources/standards/ncte-ira-standards-for-the-english-language-arts/

National Council of Teachers of Mathematics (NCTE). (n.d.). *Principles, standards, and expectations*. Nctm.org. Retrieved on November 11, 2022, from https://www.nctm.org/Standards-and-Positions/Principles-and-Standards/Principles,-Standards,-and-Expectations/

Neubauer, D., & Fradella, H. (2017). *America's courts and the criminal justice system*. Cengage Learning.

Payne, R. (2019). *A framework for understanding poverty: A cognitive approach*. aha! Process.

Postema, G. J. (1986). *Bentham and the common law tradition* 207 17, 266 311.

Sandler, C., & Keefe, J. (2009). *Legal words you should know*. Adams Media.

Sandwick, T., Wonsun Hahn, J., & Hassoun Ayoub, L., (2019). Fostering community, sharing power: Lessons for building restorative justice school cultures. *Education Policy Analysis Archives, 27*(145). https://doi.org/10.14507/epaa.27.4296

Seale, C. (2020). *Thinking like a lawyer: A framework for teaching critical thinking to all students*. Routledge.

Telson, E. R., & McDonald, S. (1992). Peer mediation among high school students: A test of effectiveness. *Social Work in Education, 14(2)*, 86–94.

Turnuklu, A., Kacmaz, T., Sunbul, D., & Ergul, H., (2009). Does peer-mediation really work? Effects of conflict resolution and peer-mediation training on high school students' conflicts. *World Conference on Educational Sciences, 2009*, 630–638.

Warters, B. (2022). *Conflict resolution education connection, CREDucation Project*. Peer mediation—Conflict resolution education connection (creducation.net). Retrieved October 24, 2022.

Weiss, J., & Mcguinn, P. (2016). States as change agents under ESSA. *Phi Delta Kappen, 97*(8), 28–33. https://doi.org/10.1177/0031721716647015

Wong, H., & Wong, R. (2018a). *The first days of school: How to be an effective teacher*. Harry K. Wong Publications.

Wong, H., & Wong, R. (2018b). *The classroom management book* (2nd ed.). Harry K. Wong Publications.

APPENDIX

MCKINNEY DISTRICT COURT
CLASSROOM WARRANT

PLAINTIFF(S) (Last Name, First Name)
V.
DEFENDANT(S) (Last Name, First Name)
REPORT DATE AND TIME:
DATE AND TIME OF INCIDENT:
SUMMARY OF INCIDENT:
WITNESSES FOR THE PLAINTIFF:
REQUESTED CLAIM:

"I'll See You in Court" Supporting Social Justice, Diversity, Equity, and Critical Thinking Through Classroom Management and Discipline in Urban Schools, pages 53–56.
Copyright © 2023 by Information Age Publishing
www.infoagepub.com
All rights of reproduction in any form reserved.

MCKINNEY DISTRICT COURT
CLASSROOM DOCKET

CASE: PLAINTIFF V. DEFENDANT
LAWYER(S) FOR PLAINTIFF:
LAWYER(S) FOR DEFENDANT:
COURT DATE:
JUDGE ASSIGNED:

REFLECTION SHEET

1. Explain (in detail) what happened?
2. How did this make you feel?
3. Could you have reacted differently? If so, how?
4. How do you think you made Dr. McKinney feel?
5. What's your plan of action so that this does not occur again?
Student Signature
Date
Teacher_

THERE IS SO MUCH TEACHING AND LEARNING TO ACCOMPLISH!
SAMPLE CLASSROOM JOBS

Job	Responsibility
Errand Runner	Responsible for running any errands for the teacher (e.g., attendance, lunch count)
Private Secretary	My "Go To" Student. Responsible for filing Reflection Sheets and Classroom Conduct Notices. Informs me when I need more copies of each.
Fire Marshall	Responsible for making sure all windows are closed, the lights are out, and the door is closed. Last person out of the classroom.
Door Greeter	Greets any visitor that comes to our classroom. His/her desk is situated by the classroom door.
Librarian	Keeps our classroom library organized. Responsible for keeping track of when students "checks out" books.
Magistrate	Responsible for collecting fees and issuing warrants. Is also responsible for organizing active warrants based on dates submitted.
Bailiff	Keeps order in our Classroom Court
Chill Out Officer	Keeps order in our Chill Out area.
Floor Officer	Issues tickets when students leave trash around their desk area.
Desk Officer	Issues tickets when students have a messy desk.
Teacher's Desk Organizer	Keeps the teacher's desk organized.
Bankers	In charge of McKinney's Savings and Loans Bank.
Store Clerks	Salesclerks
Lottery Workers	Salesclerks
Line Leader	Leads the line when we are in the hallway.
Lunchroom Table Cleaner	Washes lunch table.
Learning Center Organizer	Organizes our learning center.
Board Cleaner	Responsible for cleaning board.
New Student Pal	Introduces the new student to our class, our rules, and procedures.
Paper Collector	Collects student papers.
Gardener	Water and takes care of our plants in the classroom.
Tech Assistant	Assists students who are having trouble with their computer/technology.
Materials Officer	Issues tickets to those students who do not bring all of their needed materials to class.
Striker	Keeps a notebook of the strikes that were issued each day.
Table Organizer	Organizes the teaching table.
Handyman	Fixes things that break in the classroom and calls the custodian for help if needed.

SAMPLE JOB APPLICATION

Date:
Name:
Address:
City/State:
Phone Number:
Job You Are Applying For:
What special skills, knowledge, and/or attitudes and experiences will assist you in meeting success as this job?
References:
Name:
Relationship:
Name:
Relationship:

SAMPLE CLASSROOM CONDUCT NOTICE

Date:

Dear , (Parent/Guardian's Name).

(Child's Name)_____ usually has a great day of teaching and learning in my class. However, today he/she received 3 strikes (I had to speak to him/her at least 3 times) for breaking our classroom rules. Checked below are the rules that were not followed today.

(List Your Classroom Rules)

___ Show respect for yourself, your peers, your teacher, and your materials.

___Raise your hand for permission if you need to leave your seat.

___ Listen, without interruptions, when others are speaking.

___Complete all classwork assignments.

___Have all needed materials for class.

 Please speak to your child about the importance of following our classroom rules, and that it interrupts the learning process for his peers. I am positive that will have a better day tomorrow!

Teacher Signature

Parent Signature

Student Signature

Printed in the United States
by Baker & Taylor Publisher Services